TRILOGY

TED PEARSON

TRILOGY

SPUYTEN DUYVIL
New York City

Excerpts from "Coptic Light" appeared in *Creative Flight* (India).

"When cutting an axe handle with an axe,
the model is surely at hand."

—Lu Chi

I. GEOMANCY

Coptic Light

"The idea is distributed in space."
—Anton Webern

1.

The irises came up early that year. Those who had shelter ventured out, while the mad were lost in the silence of others whose faith in reason was marred by doubt. No madder than most, you chose to roam. But, as the sun rose higher each day, your thoughts kept turning home. Despair pervaded a somber palette of desolated shades. These, in turn, became wards of the streets and languished where once they had played.

2.

Imagine a new world rendered by time into nothing fit for the old. From whence you wandered through an arid waste where the wind ran hot and cold. Your quest began with a Sibylline dare. And while each day ended in time for the next, reversals of fortune were common fare. Self-possession became an obsession. As did your taste for the angel's share. You have pledged yourself to your gods and your dreams, but in fact you owe them nothing.

3.

We interrupt work on this his tomb to attend to the demiurge. Nothing lasts forever. Such were his final words. The afterlife itself depends on the legions of faithful departed. Those whose bare lives illustrate how the myth of heaven started. Thus are forged the lies that bind, which raises the problem of other minds. And, though our words bespeak our resistance, we're no less other to ourselves and no less bound for inexistence.

4.

Learn to write what you want to read, to paraphrase B. B. King. The
very stuff of your desire is shaped by the words you sing. Few roads are
closed to your endless quest, though most lead nowhere fast. Of the ten
thousand forms, there is no one measure, though each is built to last.
Your lyrics issue from your inner voices. Compañeros in the Theater of
Selves. Which is where we found you rehearsing songs you wrote on the
road to hell.

5.

As spring nights yielded to summer days, the trail of the Grail seemed
clearer. But what if our memories faded away, and friends we thought
we'd never forget disappeared in the rear-view mirror? A wise man
compared reality to the blind eye that taught us to stare. We fixed our
gaze on a single word as if all worlds were there. Suddenly, a mirage
appeared that seemed to foreshadow our future. One which links the
distant past and the present to which it's been sutured.

6.

History attaches to mental landscapes, reflecting such changes as time
has wrought. The doors of perception stand open and empty. Memories
of past lives leave you distraught. One sure thing is that no one abides
when their body and mind part ways. Once, bright moments turned back
the clock. Now, they no longer light your days. So, why not abandon
your idle reflections? Look for a thought you can trust. Without being
precipitate, to live and die as one must.

7.

Doubt intervenes between damaged dreams and desires from beyond
the pale. There are gaps in space and lapses in time where we are bound
to fail. By all accounts, you say what you mean. And it's not impossible
you mean it. That's a discussion for another day, which isn't to demean
it. The Grail we seek is the Grail you sought. We, who dwell at the roots
of things, and whose words are the flowers of thought.

8.

These songs speak to power, if only at three removes. But who's to say
our faith in song will survive what the evidence proves? The sparest of
melodies once sustained us. The silence that followed now constrains
us. We've searched for the Grail, high and low. To what precise end,
we'll never know. Clueless we were. And clueless remain. Our quest has
assumed a life of its own, at whose dark purposes we guess in vain.

9.

Background noises vex our peripheries. Seekers of knowledge distrust
epiphanies. The past brings updates that reprove us. "We see we saw not
what did move us." In fact, we sing as others pray, but only to the Void
that lies beyond the waiting grave. No good end is above suspicion. On
our quest, we've seen the attrition. Meanwhile, actuaries number our
days. As their sums diminish, we fade away.

10.

Death is latent in the body proper, beyond which lies a barren scape with unsuspected depths. Lost souls line its byways and moan with every breath. After donning their self-styled masks, they go about their appointed tasks. They were monads looking to improve their lives, but their analytics faltered. Now, they number countless dead and miles of roadside altars.

11.

That which eyes cannot not see constitutes the visible. And even as it has shaped our lives, our quest may well be risible. Still we persist, despite the laughter of ghosts who know just what comes after. But why not clasp a stranger's hand where native flowers make their stand and bloom on unmarked graves. Where every other loved one was the one we couldn't save, we can but count our losses and learn to rue the day.

12.

Abandon all hope was the Party slogan. Far from sanguine, it cut like a blade. Acrid smoke rose from an igneous heap in a landscape peopled by shades. As the sky glowed red with clouds of fire, the threat to our days in the sun was dire. Rumor has it the Grail was polished by the writhings of the damned. Whose writings, since passed down to us, are now in great demand.

13.

Our quest began with an invitation to sail uncharted seas. Eager to flee domestication, we caught a westering breeze. On we sailed in spite of the hazards – *because* of the hazards – we knew not where. We heard the strains of a freedom song upon the dissembling air. It seemed the dawn of a brand new day; instead it marked the end, they say. That's when the storm, with winds unchecked, drove us without mercy toward the shoals on which we wrecked.

14.

The darker the dream, the deeper the debt. What life can't forgive, it never forgets. Anonyms essayed our former domain and sang the plight of bodies in pain. How we got *here* is anyone's guess. Our nights are bleak; our days depressed. The future comprises our doubts in waiting. They stand revealed in the light that's fading. With the sun occluded, the sky grew black. And thunder gave lightning the depth it had lacked.

15.

Exiled to lands that time forgot, you set your watch by the sun. Your only thought was refuge from a life lived on the run. You've had enough of wizards and witches. There were rivers to cross, but damned few bridges. Rapids quickened the passage of time. Reason balked at the end of the line, where an ill wind whipped through a high-walled canyon, and disaster beckoned as if by design.

16.

Last call finds you nodding off. Daybreak threatens from afar. For now, there's you and the night and the music. And an uptown trio in a downtown bar. "Not my poem. Mr. Steinway's poem." You dread the thought of heading home. Only ghosts await you there. And cracks in the ceiling at which you stare. Thirty-six black keys and fifty-two white. And one last cadenza to end the set and usher you into the night.

17.

Death waits on the far shore. Life is an unchecked wave. It slowly builds until its crests, then breaks and crests no more. Seeking shelter, for which you yearn, few signs point the way. Thus, the low-ghost at break of day. But signs there are, and they're waiting to be read. Your pain is proof that you're not dead. In fact, you're ready to carry on, now that your limits have been redrawn.

18.

With few stars and no moon, ground fog thickens around the lagoon while distant sirens drown the cry of a loon. A seaside chapel's psalmodies calm the night's anomalies. And suddenly it's you there, from sleep unfurled, standing in the predawn chill at your window on the world. Where you wait on the rising sun and muse on the changes about to come, hoping thus to take your ease should dreams become realities.

19.

Saturnine nights. Irrational numbers. Recurring nightmares that plague your slumber. Voyeurs want the money shot. A memento mori forgets you not. Your waking hours pass the time it takes to measure your decline. Self-doubt holds off affirmations by taking refuge in abnegation. Proof of concept has become your credo. Thus to account for the sundry symptoms that vie to survive your veto.

20.

The gods of song were mute when asked to confirm their end was at hand. History tells us time stood still when the last band died on the stand. Desire conditioned our affects. Our sorrow gave us pause. Reason speaks to no effect if death is the final cause. Consider this a threnody that isn't sung in vain. Their albums are proof those gods existed. Whose music soothes our pain.

21.

Life without end is an aberrant dream. It threatens death's finality and any peace that brings. Probability aids stability, but necromancy is more my thing. This I've learned in pursuit of the Grail, a task at which I expect to fail. Form shapes purpose, and purpose meaning. Not for nothing is seeming believing. Whence comes the Void to which we aspire. The source of all form and the seat of desire.

22.

In the welcome calm of a windless day, life doesn't so much burden age as parcel out what time remains. Memories fade with the morning mist. Fragments of half-forgotten tunes recur in random gists. The prospect of beauty in its latest guise mocks our sorrow at our own demise. Infirmity defines our pace, yet we move with remembered grace. Lived life speaks to where we've been. Its words the sole remaining trace.

23.

At the end of the dance, the end of the Real. What little we know of it shapes what we feel. Meanwhile, we trust in what comes next to keep our dreams alive. Thus, to resist the second thoughts of introspective jive. "The self is no mystery," wrote the sage who staked his honor on the written page. Whenever old words join with new, both are prized by the welcome few.

24.

Where a waxing gibbous bade farewell, a blood moon greeted your arrival. It was time to leave once cherished haunts. Time to address your needs and wants. Against the day you fail to wake, you rise to greet the sun. Since the death of meaning is the meaning of death, you rehearse the ghost you'll soon become. Where the only sound is a cosmic hum and the only symbol an empty sign, the Grail you seek is nothing less than the poem at the end of time.

Gnossiennes

"Ideas are substitutes for grief."
—Marcel Proust

1.

Regarding our place
           in worldly affairs,
                      it is said there is
a place apart, else-
           where than it was
                      thought to be. Thus,
the mystery and
           strangeness of
                      the world, not least
in its particulars.

2.

Once we slipped
           the bonds of thought,
                      there was no end
to thinking. The force
           that authors all
                      that lives sustains
the dance of all
           that lasts. It's
                      Fate that guides
the shooter's hand
           until the dice are cast.

3.

Are we or are we
              not determined?
                            Will, as such, will
not suffice to find
              these songs a home.
                            Beyond which
chance and the forces
              of mammon align
                            to serve ends
not one's own.

4.

If character is fate,
              it's also the case
                            that our demons
are products of our
              own devising. Their
                            lamentations are
beyond compare.
              And when we're
                            alone, we're alone
together, never
              knowing whether
                            our desires are
truly ours or theirs.

5.

Where rhapsodes
          sang of heroic
                    deeds, as we now
write of quotidian
          needs, they thereby
                    entered history.
Even as one word
          follows another,
                    verses follow where
sound forms lead.
          Let these lines,
                    if soundly
wrought, sing
          in praise of
                    sound as thought.

6.

Mondrian wrote
          of color that
                    "relation is
the principal
          thing." This is also
                    true for language,
whose subtle syntax
          can be sung with grace.
                    Such that we,
in relation to others,
          seek, as they do,
                    to find our place.

7.

Being *is not* and
        yet *there is* being.
                Humans arrived,
belated as ever,
        a folly of Nature
            whose infinite
power we have
        sought to bend
            to our will. This
has become our
        defining trait.
            Hubris alone
has sealed our fate.

8.

Experience resides
        where memory abides.
            Thus, our experiments,
regardless of outcome,
        only add to our memory's
            sum. Hence,
whatever we think
        to build, we've
            barely just begun.
"One doesn't make
        just any experiment,
            but does what
must be done."

9.

To discourse is
            to wander,
                        which leads us
to digress. What
            happens happens
                        only in the telling,
even as all things
            are strictly defined
                        by the forms they
dare to inhabit.

10.

It's only when
            we occupy the present
                        that the past can
be said to have had
            a future. In our
                        waking lives, we do
what we can. In dreams,
            we restore what time's
                        undone – *off* the clock
and *in* the moment –
            where what's been said
                        were better sung.

11.

Body and soul,
          in chromatic splendor,
                    rehearse the song
of the embodied mind.
          Given the weight
                    of the verb *to be*,
we only become
          what we are
                    in time. All things
are known by
          the forms that
                    define them
and the names
          we call them by.

12.

Every night, you
          leave off writing,
                    only to resume
at break of day.
          Years later, and
                    the end's in sight.
Given that one must
          write regardless.
                    Given, the available
means are few. Given,
          we abide in the
                    silence of others.
Given, that
          there remains
                    much to do.

13.

If only because
          they abhor a vacuum,
                    constraints give rise
to a kind of freedom.
          An illusion, perhaps,
                    but no more so
than your other
          enabling myths.
                    Fatalism may be
another illusion,
          if not an actual
                    symptom. One
that makes us
          the hapless heirs
                    of history's myriad
victims.

14.

Every concession
          is a diminution,
                    not least those
we make to age.
          But we weren't
                    wrong to persist
in living. Despite
          the myths of heaven
                    and hell, death
is as final as it is
          unforgiving.

15.

Meaning is as
              meaning does
                        in the act of
making meaning.
              So what does it
                        mean to make
a poem? And where
              else might its
                        meaning reside
if not in the act
              of its making? Thus
                        to admonish those
who imagine that
              meaning is here
                        for the taking.

16.

Between mute speech
              and a steadfast gaze,
                        the reader seeks
out new unknowns.
              We say we see and
                        speak for ourselves,
though the words we hear
              are not our own. Hence,
                        it should come
as no surprise
              when the music of
                        language signifies
that to read a poem
              is to hear with eyes.

Impromptus

"It is signs that realize Ideas."
—Gilles Deleuze

1.

Words emerge from the silence that surrounds them. It is their fate to embody that silence, to which they will return.

2.

The poet wove a thousand threads to invoke a singular sum: "I found the words for every thought / I ever had – but One."

3.

The history of diffidence began with a qualm. Subject to one simple rubric: Think much. Speak little. Write less, if at all.

4.

Our elders lived in a habitable world, albeit it was dying. And even now we close our eyes to a fact beyond denying.

5.

Despite its propensity for false promises, we greet each dawn *as if* the sun would bring a brighter day.

6.

Privation is best endured in solitude. Sacrifice stems from the myth of a
self that exists as such to be squandered.

7.

Time reveals the arrogance of achievement. With only the barest
essentials on hand, there's yet more work to be done.

8.

The truth assumes each and every risk, including its negation. And, to
live is to share that risk, the only truth we know.

9.

In time, the truth of truth might fail. Which would bring to an end our
lifelong quest for the poem we call our Grail.

10.

Bare life dares not hope to thrive. Those who succeed us are on their
own – a victory of sorts that none survive.

11.

Memory rehearses a life of regret. The pain we've caused, the pain we've endured, and the pain we can't forget.

12.

The poem of a life is a suite of contingencies. One which welcomes any chance to escape bare life's amenities.

13.

White nights light the darkest hours, through which we persist. In time, creation becomes negation. Ceasing to suffer, we cease to exist.

14.

Laughter imparts the truth of existence. Curiosity led to original sin. The mythic portals of paradise mark where exile and death begin.

15.

Experience teaches what it knows. Then you turn the page. The young are ever new to youth as are the old to age.

16.

To be alive is to pay the price for all that's gone before. Although, before
your debt is called, life demands yet more.

17.

An inner fire burns bright in some, even as its light reveals they're yet to
be what they might become.

18.

Words and music must be as one if song is to survive. Embodied in the
singer's voice, words and music thrive.

19.

The more you come to resemble yourself, the harder to tell you apart.
Yet, it's the difference between you that has kept you alone from the start.

20.

Music animates bodies at rest. Dancers count their beats. To write is to
follow the words we are given, even to the verge of defeat.

21.

Transient beauty illumines what advancing age concedes. It's one thing
to know what follows. Another to go where it leads.

22.

Mutability shapes the bitter end that beauty's form proposes. Ideals are
static fantasies which living art opposes.

23.

Poetry thrives on its contradictions – its losses, leaps, and lapses. These
rely on formal means to render fresh synapses.

24.

At best, life lasts for decades. Art beyond all measure. It follows that a
life in art should all the more be treasured.

II. AFTER DARK

Prologues

"The sign of identity is a relative term."
—Willard Van Orman Quine

1.

As death is the sum of its metaphors,
a life is the tenor of its days.

Slowly, a blank page fills with words,
the only words you know.

The syntax is that of a sorrow song
you learned a lifetime ago.

2.

A bed, a desk, a dresser, and a bookshelf.
A stack of records and a radio.

A room with windows facing south
and east, overlooking a patio.

Such was the room where you woke at dawn
to the rising sun and the robin's song.

3.

Faded images blur your childscape
amid the tree-shaded lawns of home.

A world of tracts and cul-de-sacs,
whose cookie-cutter blocks you roamed.

After years among the living dead,
dreams of city life filled your head.

4.

What does it mean to *enter* history? Where
in those endless battalions were you?

A nameless extra in a Pyrrhic victory thinks
Of the excluded and the fortunate few.

The past marks the start of our present decline.
The future disdains what we've left behind.

5.

On family outings, you weighed the merits
of an era's roadside attractions.

Then one day, it wasn't your father,
but you behind the wheel.

How else explain the woman beside you,
clearly not your mother?

6.

History begins with the body's memory
of places and faces obscured by time.

The endless days of summer disguise
the change that signals youth's demise.

Now, it's winter in a hellish land where
exiles dwell among the damned.

7.

A stranger asks, "Do you want to touch me?"
in a voice that's been through hell. And it's

not the person, but their need that speaks,
one which you recognize all too well.

You, who are no less needful and alone,
curse the streets that once were home.

8.

Alone at a bus stop, you watch young lovers
embrace in the streetlight's muted glow.

Their passion reminds you of nights long ago
when such moments shaped your fate.

The lovers are lost in a world of their own.
The bus is running late.

9.

Remote from any but the one tradition,
your words assemble themselves at will.

Their forms are many; their motives few.
Their battle flags are black and blue.

They can conjure ghosts at the turn of a phrase,
not least the absent author of their days.

10.

The text is rife with grammatical persons,
of which *they* are but one.

From embodied minds, embodied words,
enough to fill a wordless scroll.

What is lost to language is lost to itself.
The text proceeds as if it were whole.

11.

His lifelong love of the music of words
was the source of his serenity.

Who parceled out the roles he played
in pursuit of nonidentity.

Now, when friends begin reminiscing,
he's the only one who's missing.

12.

Seeking more than the life you knew,
you discovered the life of the mind.

You learned to play the music of words
whose meanings accrue over time.

That's when the beauty of truth's austerity
exposed the truth of beauty's precarity.

Night Sounds

"The who will always be the face of the what."
—Michel Deguy

1.

Every beginning is a new beginning and bespeaks an end in itself. *A lone star appeared in the midnight sky above the sleeping city.* The poetry of silence is a kind of language. *A density of lights defined the skyline, thinning toward the suburbs.* Where prose is fixed on the far horizon, verse traces the contours of the land. *A loner by nature, he hated crowds.* Language shapes the words in our heads. *Once dawn broke, he took to his bed.*

2.

That the wicked would prosper was once deemed a heresy, if it *was* heresy and not inspiration. *His legacy consisted of countless hours in which he did next to nothing.* Even the King of Fools needs a laugh, such is the burden of his crown. *His thoughts were fleeting because they feared what would happen to them if they stayed.* It is said that the clever ones think on their feet, but where do the sleepless dream?

3.

In order to thrive, one must first survive, but you can only tread so much water. *He faithfully followed the words he was given, even as they led into exile.* As surely as one wave follows another, the horizon recedes to infinity. *Rhythmic patterns sanctioned his days, which he passed in the arms of solitude.* Night enshrouds the aging poet in a preview of what's to come. *His books were illumined by the light of disaster.* "Crusoe," we say, "was 'rescued.'"

4.

At the heart of the problem lies a world of multiplicities. What problem? Whose world? *In his exile, he was foreign, even to himself.* Words appear on the x-axis, where magic is said to reside. *He spent his days on impossible choices.* What little we know of the universe is what we're given to see. *He saw a world of precarity and dreamt of one at peace.*

5.

Redacted pages suspend the narrative. Moments of silence sustain the song. *He wrote at length of midnight's role in the slow dismantling of his dreams.* Verbs put in motion what nouns announce. The act precedes the action. *Where one solution was dissolution, he imagined the world without him.* A text and its author are soon parted. The difference sparks the reader's gaze. *His was an art of contingency, good till the end of days.*

6.

We seem to make every finite thing a hieroglyph of the infinite – and hope such correspondences might heal these mortal wounds. *His thoughts deployed from the liminal state in which he woke to the world.* Poems aspire to the condition of poetry, around which lesser motives swirl. *In private moments, he gazed with pleasure at the books that line his shelves.* The infinite, too, will attain its end, empty of all but itself.

7.

Balmy air on windless nights is almost paradisal. *Under the light of a strawberry moon, he began his next recital.* First come the bitter hypotheses of childhood. Then come the monsters that steal our sleep. *He bore the scars of grave misfortunes, invisible though they remained.* Adolescence follows with its reckless predations, under the twin stars of lust and freedom. *Loved or unloved, it hardly mattered. He walked the streets alone.*

8.

Knowledge of self is no small thing, not least that the self is a fiction. *His very name was a figure of loss, as was the work that claimed it.* Whatever is subject to these explanations has little cause to rejoice. *He stared with longing at the mute particulars he once had given voice.* Sooner or later, our truths depart for the barrens of disbelief. *Hence, as the final silence approached, he was ever more hesitant to speak.*

9.

Even when we lose our way, words take our measure, day by day. *His words were rare as blood from a stone, yet each was another step closer to home.* But where is home, if not where we are? Life once came from beyond the stars. *His practice detailed the abstraction of light from the darkness that surrounds us.* Whatever the future promises, the past will soon confound us. *Who took new risks with every text, lived each day to see what's next.*

10.

The search for a subject reflects our need to inhabit new paradigms. *His works were addressed, "poste restante," to the ragged edge of time.* While the old guard grazes on its storied past, futurity tells us nothing lasts. *Belated he came and defeated he went from project to project until he was spent.* How survive without a plan? "I'm sure we all do the best we can." *Even so, he refused to succumb to the memory he knew he would soon become.*

11.

In a time of reversals, we see things askew. Day for night. Wrong for right. The future familiar, as in déjà vu. *Even as the struggle for justice persists, he wondered whether justice exists.* Tradition tells us to abjure the flesh. *The embodied mind defined his quest.* Where fear of death is a common trait, *he chose instead to embrace his fate.* Some seek life beyond the grave, no matter how absurd. *He sought the poem at the end of time, where a word could at last be a word.*

12.

He learned where he was by being there. Clarity prevails, but at what cost? *Having lost his illusions, he feared for his dreams.* Facing forces beyond our ken, freedom was a matter of if, not when. *He counted being understood as the great misfortune of his life.* Of what use are platitudes in a world beset by strife? *Of all his feelings, despair alone approached what he knew to be true.* How account for the hope he felt whenever he heard the blues?

13.

As he aged, he delighted when time stood still. We begin by counting the decades to come and end up counting the hours. *Seeming to fade as the sun went down, his hopes began to sour.* We live in a time of emergent truths, which for many have yet to flower. *He likened his life to sonata form with its movements joined by sutures.* A present deaf to its history can only be blind to its future.

14.

He wandered with nothing but time on his hands, turning left three times to go right. And, while tracing these arabesques, he imagined the book he would write. The cover pictures an empty pier where melancholy thrives. But all that's left of the book to come is the book that never arrives. *He once wrote an ode on the silence of others, a lacuna he couldn't explain.* Questions were many. Answers few. Unspoken doubts are all that remain.

15.

When he lost his job as a one-man band — last hired, first fired — he watched as idioms were turned into axioms and then became cliches. Conventions map onto genres, from which they rarely stray. *In his youth, when the future beckoned, he stored these fragments against the day his mind became less fecund.* In the morning. At low tide. A rock on the beach. Half-exposed. Hard. And silent.

16.

From exile, he recalled the years he roamed his childhood streets. Life became an endless maze of lines that never meet. *Would words abet his need for song or force him to retreat?* Myriad screens feature gifs and memes, icons of devolution. *He grew detached from the world of pain, lost for a solution.* Even as the cosmos expands, and with it our human arts, its legions of bodies, great and small, grow ever farther apart.

17.

Disaster clarified his wants and needs. Multiple logics, like multiple worlds, are known by their contradictions. *Every season was a new ordeal intended to test his convictions.* We seek new modes of justice which are absent from our laws. *He sought to grasp the public mood, which often gave him pause.* Sooner or later, there will come a day when we will mourn what we knew to be true, yet remained at a loss to say.

18.

He agreed that words are "the currency of fools" and embraced his poverty. Better dismissed for seeming inept than reviled for simple honesty. *He counted his lacks as virtues. His syntax helped him survive.* Words are addressed from body to body, albeit they rarely arrive. *He treasured his solitude under the sun. He simply wanted to count as one.* They say that "the journey is truly immense," which is why, when it's over, we're done.

19.

In the end, he hoped the sum of his work exceeded expectations. Writing translates the language of thought with its many reverberations. *He wondered what posthumous life would be like among those friends who survived.* Would books suffice to bring to mind what memory failed to revive? *Night sounds flowed from his manuscript pages.* Whose lines addressed the states of things that they might speak to the ages.

20.

He liked to imagine that his travails served a worthy if uncertain end. Troubles arise when oracles speak a language we can't comprehend. *Every line he undertook was meant to stave off harm.* As soon as the low-ghost raises the dead, hierophants raise the alarm. *He asked for little – was who he was – and laughed at time's duplicity.* In seeking the past, it's last words first. A matter of more than proximity.

21.

Once dawn broke, he took to his bed. Language orders the words in our heads. *A loner by nature, he avoided crowds.* Where prose is fixed on the far horizon, verse follows the lay of the land. *A density of lights defined the skyline, thinning toward the suburbs.* The poetry of silence is its own language. *A lone star appeared in the midnight sky above the sleeping city.* Every beginning is a new beginning and bespeaks an end in itself.

Endnotes

"Every message calls the code into question."
—Umberto Eco

Chapter 1

1. A dance made entirely of transitions.

2. Conditions in which the One and the Other present a unified facade.

3. In his notes, he refers to "the god-machine, purveyor of grand illusions."

4. A phrase mistakenly attributed to Rimbaud.

5. In a later version, "When shadows fall / theory lights its lamp."

6. Said of those whose pleasure was his pain.

7. A veiled reference to a former lover.

8. Whose loss was once the measure of his days.

Chapter 2

1. Having reached the end of a series of failures.

2. Surrender followed from utter exhaustion.

3. A rare photo shows the coming disaster.

4. All languages are equally foreign, all homelands equally
   remote.

5. His mind's eye dwells on impossible figures.

6. Said of such moments as when memory fails.

7. In a city whose moment is lost to history.

8. He fears his desires are no longer his own.

Chapter 3

1. Between sunup & sundown, paper & ink.

2. A reference to the hand that presumes to write and the
   mind that presumes to think.

3. Many articles address this question. Few have challenged
   the preeminence of sight.

4. It is here assumed that, for all we know, appearances *are*
   our reality.

5. Such is the logic enshrined in propositions.

6. Elsewhere, he defines a formal movement as a series of
   intermittent moments.

7. Thus, to reconcile words and their deeds.

8. Whose trajectories are endlessly divisible.

Chapter 4

1. The assertion of rights precedes publication.

2. Taken from a notebook spanning his teens.

3. In his youth, he haunted these rolling hills.

4. Further evidence he joined the Resistance in lieu of
monastic life.

5. His daydreams preoccupy none but himself, but they serve
him very well.

6. Ordered fragments fill a folder whose contents date to his
high-school years.

7. Thus to recall his late mother's passion for hospital corners
and starched sheets.

8. At dusk, he revisits his childhood fear of the dark and its
shapeless monsters.

Chapter 5

1. The Absurd is a comic form of humanism.

2. It now appears that he visited her the very night she died.

3. In music, this is called a deceptive cadence. In fiction, it's called a McGuffin.

4. Critics point to his glowing endorsement of her recent posthumous exhibition.

5. Telling lines in an unknown hand were added to the author's notes.

6. Not without irony, he wrote of love as the gateway to a fictive world.

7. A fragment in an abandoned essay details "the evils of active introspection."

8. Similar comments elsewhere suggest he was loath to explain himself.

Chapter 6

1. Imagination refers to the ability to think in mental images.

2. Allusive to St. Paul's praise of madness.

3. Clouds disambiguate a sheltering sky.

4. It was in this grove that Shiva appeared and whispered, "Devotion frees."

5. Melancholy dogged his nights and days.

6. The historical data is well established.

7. Pursuant to the swing and sway of syntax, where phonemes lead, morphemes follow.

8. While yet a child, he rose at dawn to watch the weather of the world.

Chapter 7

1. Synthesis appears to vacillate between its role as a desirable outcome and its status as a point of departure.

2. Given that being is essentially static, it resists all attempts at becoming.

3. Nor does it appear willing to accede to the cultural logic of ghosts.

4. In popular literature, what's considered true is what readers want most to believe.

5. Abnegation is a form of self-protection.

6. The one instance of bad faith that capped off his sense of betrayal.

7. As Raworth notes, "sub is not un." Beneath one's awareness lies a world in wait.

8. In its quest for knowledge, the West pursued a disembodied poetics.

Chapter 8

1. That summer, in a letter to L—, he blamed faulty wiring for
his lexical dilemma.

2. With respect to the current abomination, he questions the
political efficacy of art.

3. Metonyms illustrate subtractive beauty.

4. The age at which children no longer speak of themselves in
the third person.

5. He claims, with nothing left to lose, that he felt "unequi-
vocally free."

6. By *here* and *now* he means *there* and *then*.

7. Thus to affirm his faith in contingency.

8. Language acquisition begins at birth with an "infinitely
small vocabulary."

Chapter 9

1. For Leibniz, an act is indiscernible from any notion of force.

2. As when something hidden is at last laid bare.

3. But does memory exist as a distinct faculty – distinct, that
is, from remembering?

4. Note his attention to sound as sense and to silence as the
truth of sound.

5. It is not by chance that his later works are increasingly
propositional.

6. An early mentor died young, by suicide if not misadventure.

7. Signification often depends on advances in significant form.

8. Statements aren't sentences, but logical constructs that
may result from the process of *making* a statement.

Chapter 10

1. We would be remiss to disregard the erotic dimensions of his work.

2. His grasp of libidinal economy is a matter of public record.

3. His happiest hours were spent with whisky and a few imaginary friends.

4. The "heartlessness of words" disproves the myth of transparent language.

5. In fact, he found consensus coercive, which fueled his aversion to crowds.

6. An insomniac, he took no comfort in the promise of eternal rest.

7. In his view, the quest for a "true self" was nothing if not rank folly.

8. As a youth, he denounced what he understood as a highly contagious regression.

Chapter 11

1. Much has been made of his legato phrasing and preference
   for slower tempos.

2. He recalls that patience was once a virtue.

3. The caveat is to be wary of sophistries that threaten our
   capacity to act.

4. A veiled reference to the recent moratorium.

5. Between passive aggression and preemptive action, he
   preferred the understated language of thought.

6. He seems to have marveled early on at the grace of floating
   signifiers.

7. His cronies opine that his distrust of virtuosity stems from
   his hatred of cul-de-sacs.

8. In his view, that which underlies our words is the surface
   on which they appear.

Chapter 12

1. Every performative constitutes an action. "Words say nothing more than they do."

2. Nature makes us all we can be. Nurture makes us what we are.

3. This is considered a testament to his powers of observation.

4. Here, the mockingbird's sprezzatura is a figure for lyric grace.

5. Invented idioms are inverted axioms. Readers are either shaken or stirred.

6. Madness follows from two distinct models: an exceptional state or a failed one.

7. Where Freud insisted negation is repression, the poet affirms it as the only way forward.

8. His later works address the present as if it had already happened.

III. Valences

Chaconne

"Poems are the epitaphs of dead languages."
—Jacques Roubaud

1.

The question was never whether but how.
The answer surpassed our understanding.
White nights canceled dreams of oblivion.

Frigid digits brought a light dusting.
Pay-per-view followed the Fall Offensive
to the rebels' base of operations.

Feral phonemes pronounced sentences.
Then, we did penance at the justice factory.
Aging docents lost us in the mazes,

but no one offered to show us the door.
In other news, tone-deaf diction has
altered the tenor of public discourse.

Your Weekly Reader is now a digitized
set of simulated reading experiences.
When virtual hands turn virtual pages,

virtual readers mime comprehension.
Virtual catharsis? Enter your password.
But the season for reason was past.

Winter solstice arrived as a gift. Lovers
made short work of the day. Then rocked
steady on the midnight shift.

2.

Silence speaks volumes in our absence.
Negative outcomes under ice-blue skies remind
first-timers to breathe when they dream.

Human speech arrives as an afterthought.
It says what it thinks we meant it to say.
In summarizing this grand experiment,

we note how cultures pass in time,
and, as our languages become extinct,
there's no one to eulogize the losses.

How join the one and the indivisible
when one is obliged to remain invisible
in order to thrive as a multiple of one?

Still more elusive is the steely syntax
with which the poet admonished peers
for dismissing their mother tongue.

He made his mark and died forthwith.
Hence, the biography now in production
begins with his early years on the road

and ends when he arrives at Parnassus,
where, for the elders, he quietly read
from his posthumous *Book of the Dead*.

3.

Recognition stems from prior knowledge.
Starting from nowhere with nothing to say,
a medley of themes passes over in silence.

I recall stout latches on a worker's lunch-
box and a jacket stuffed with paperbacks
meant for lunchtime reading.

Wine-stained pages told of wine-dark seas.
These, so they say, are tales of the ancients,
whose poets made them immortal.

Now that you know you have options,
feel free to commingle sense and sound
and follow them to higher ground.

Meanwhile, people died for nothing
while bad faith clung to the liminal state
that reeks of injustice and dark truths

the living are loath to reveal. Harsh
edicts opened fresh wounds, but the diva's
recital was as balm to the afflicted. Her

rich contralto seduced us all with her
artful renditions of homegrown classics
from the songbook she was born to sing.

4.

No less eager to touch than to be touched,
lust is a monument to youth's despair.
All sales are final. All relations doomed.

A cloud secures your lasting impressions.
Each image, recurring to vigilance,
takes up a pose on history's doormat.

Duration plots the human quandary,
less than a period, more than an age.
Imagine the sum of earthly life as

a smokebreak for canonical authors,
leaving no time to spare for a cocktail
or to gloss the wisdom of the ages.

Wisdom to which we're unlikely to add.
But consider the organs that bring us
pleasure and have done now for years.

We, too, are eager to touch and
to be touched, even as we now turn
to embrace in the welcome dark –

hoping to conjure there our much
younger selves, lost as they are,
and sacred as they are, to memory.

5.

Smooth sailing wasn't easy to come by.
We shared our travails as we mapped the coast.
Motile gambits gave nerves carte blanche.

These are examples of what we're after.
Later, we'll come back and stitch them up.
That's how the living become exempla.

And so we'll proceed, without sentiment.
Crime scene photos are as stark as it gets.
Much like prose that awaits your verdict,

symmetry tips well and smiles good evening.
Now, having entered a fictive universe,
the exempla are eager to come back to life.

Tales of resurrection notwithstanding,
everything is back in working order,
even as the number of readers declines.

Angelic spawn write curious stories,
in which almost anything *could* happen,
but almost nothing ever does.

Time travel poses a formal problem.
In case of emergency, you're on your own.
Hereafter, let the *isms* be damned.

6.

It was a matter of musicianship, of
growth by subtraction, a chance meeting
between minor thirds and a flurry

of notes in arpeggiated wonder. And
wonder indeed is all we recalled as
eulogies echoed from the high pulpit.

Then, with nary a soupçon of doubt,
we confirmed base units of pure substance
as true measures of molecular mass.

Granted, that episode *was* a challenge.
We aren't always hungry for knowledge.
In fact, we would love some ceviche.

The wake (which we attended) was
catered. Morbid fascination had led us
there. That, and we were hungry.

Dinner was followed by an all-night jam.
Ghosts appeared to assert their mastery.
Though too few listened, the great dead

spoke of our most intimate desires.
Those which have served to define us
and the music to which we aspire.

7.

The primality of One, which is no
mere integer, will make no concessions
to those who would exclude it.

Albeit the many take refuge in numbers,
weaponized data precludes their advance.
And that comes straight from the top.

As your pleasure wanes, your desire
wanders. While you were dodging thought
balloons, the magus raised the stakes.

Those who expected to die for glory
must have thought they were living a dream
from which there would be no waking.

Meanwhile, back at the make-work factory,
traumatic kernels have been retooled to ensure
yet another wrongful outcome in the Land

of Wrongful Outcomes. Let's begin
with the suppression of rights and what
it would take to reclaim them.

How is contingent on *if* and *when*, which
in turn are contingent on who's asking and
who sets the odds on our walking away.

8.

The following poem was made from scratch.
If you can read it, thank a teacher.
And, if not, how hard did you really try?

Clearly, we don't all swoon over poetry.
Which isn't what he said. He said, "No
one *listens* to poetry." But, if they did,

they'd understand its need to mock
the automatisms into which the language
has fallen. Only now do we reckon

our losses. Only now do we dare imagine
the end of meaning as we know it.
Of course, we're determined to finish

what we started. A bit of shopping.
A bite of lunch. Then, we'll catch a bus
for home and get right back to work.

Seasonal light can provoke old ghosts.
Production is steady, rain or shine.
Timeless the poem at the end of time.

And timely the song the low-ghost
sings, announcing now that winter's
past, it might as well be spring.

9.

In a year marked by catastrophe,
precarity became pandemic. Never
safe from capital's predations,

workers fell into abject poverty.
Then, in a parody of social death,
people began feeling short of breath.

The tyrant sucked up all the air.
And given his every word was a lie,
his every inhalation drained life

from the polis. It hurts to recall those
who suffered and died to build a workers'
paradise. Which *this* assuredly is not.

Nor do we expect one to suddenly
appear, welcome as it surely would be.
We're still looking for a living wage,

affordable housing, a four-day work
week, and decent healthcare for all.
Life after capitalism will be worth

the wait. As will thinking beyond
the dialectic – that insatiable, if
all but mythic, three-headed beast.

10.

Wise words temper cunning speech acts.
The graveyard gives us home-field advantage
Where fluorescent placards tout cartoon life.

So when is a statement not a sentence?
We sought the truth by the Hunter's Moon.
But how decide among undecidables?

Necessity offered shelter to the poet.
The only condition was that it be
purposeful. *It* being that which we see

as our practice. *That* being strictly our
duty of care. Dimensionless voids
host graven images. Odalisques line

the highway to hell. Ghost music
echoes down the corridor of years.
Imagine the power we concede

to memory – sufficient to join
or sunder the memorious and that
which they choose to recall.

Last night, I went to the dead zone.
Forgotten faces sought recognition.
Forgotten names lived cartoon lives.

11.

Poems leave off wherever they will,
only to begin again. The poet's life
is attuned to those rhythms, which

hold him captive to the waiting page.
There his closest readers find him,
waiting for the next discrepant word

while honing every line. The question
isn't why poetry is difficult. In fact,
it often is, but what worthwhile is not?

If life itself is difficult, so, too, is love.
And still we persist in living and
loving and take each day in stride.

Interpretations may be weak or strong.
The best are those that translate us
between and among our languages.

The poem is subject to variant readings,
but the text remains the same. It is no
more difficult than it needs to be if you

grant the autonomy it seeks. Though
"words say nothing more than they do,"
if you let them, they'll do what they say.

12.

Where, when, and under what circumstances?
How far? How long? And what was she thinking
when she called out to Orpheus from Hades?

She knew that he'd turn and then bear the guilt.
Hence, her affair with the Lord of the Dead
could continue and she'd be held blameless.

This was the work of her Bad Boy Syndrome,
a not uncommon fetish. And, if only the gods
weren't gossips, no one would be the wiser.

That's the thing about origin myths.
They do but mask much older myths,
whose unmasked eyes are mirrored orbs

concealing an abyss. It's there you'll find
the origin of origins, simple ciphers that
set the stage for our present devolution.

One says turtles all the way down.
Another says listen to the wind that howls,
seeking to become articulate.

In by ear. Out as song. A fiction spun
of dark matter, which, like us, will not be
found in the annotated history of time.

13.

What, short of death, might free us
from a life immured in the present?
Even if you wanted to be everywhere

at once, time has long since buggered
the threads on *that* pipe dream for good.
Simply put, one would rather *live*

in the moment than *be* in the present,
which is life in a rear-facing mirror.
Let's consider comets and dandelions.

The rocks hew to their orbits. Blossoms
follow the prevailing winds. Hence, there's
either a plot or a tell. That is, a *telos*.

So why not tell us about this obsession
with the past of your immanent desire.
Based on your growing dissatisfaction,

be it resolved that the present exists
to sell you a future that will never happen.
It can only dissolve in your presence

as the sum of repeated disappointments.
Which is never true of life in the moment,
for as long as the moment lasts.

14.

If not a lullaby, perhaps a flight
of whisky. If not a quartet, perhaps
a grand piano. A brief discourse

on free will follows. To sleep or not to
sleep. That is the issue. Its resolution is
above my pay grade. As are the sullen

thoughts that complicate my nights.
What clarities remain are scarce comfort
in the blinding light of sunrise. Even as

I think to start my day, last night's
dreamscape was too familiar, too close
to everyday life, but for one detail.

The unthinkable had happened,
and we were living in the aftermath.
Famine and disease would soon

finish off survivors of the last world war,
which was fought over food and water.
Now, on waking to each day's terrors,

we search the morning sky for portents, of
which there are plenty, but none bode
well for our fate in the coming extinction.

15.

People have died here for no good reason.
Others lost themselves and couldn't be found.
What bitter wind will serve to revive them?

What magic make them as they once were?
Only the necromancer knows the lyrics
which tell the timeless hunger of the dead.

Dissociation remained an option.
He, who didn't have to be here, wasn't.
Never mind the prints he left behind.

But, you have to feel it to believe it,
"it" being the embodied presence of
the last best thought you'll ever have.

Age makes wrinkles in the fabric of time.
We bear the face and gait of its passing.
Time bears the full dimensions of our years.

Infinity shares a space-time riddle
which one, being mortal, cannot explain.
Mineral facts are unassailable.

Speech production requires some effort.
False prophets crowd the airwaves.
Absolute freedom is an absolute lie.

16.

Better to stand here, naked and foolish,
than to cloak oneself in abnegation
as the mavens of poetry would have it.

Why, they ask, must you be so difficult?
Life, they argue, is tough enough.
True fans like to recognize the tune.

Where finger exercises dance across the
keyboard, etudes test your interpretive skills.
And true adepts harbor musical values,

many of which pertain to poetry.
There are but two impediments: words
and their disparate meanings.

Why, indeed, must it be so difficult
if not to separate readers from tourists?
And besides, "No one listens to poetry."

Sometimes, though, a density of matter
appears and assumes a form we can live
with. *That* is sufficient cause to proceed.

Where structure sustains the text in situ,
the reader animates every word,
and the poet is nowhere to be seen.

17.

In what immemorial season did
the legendary lovers part? For what
half-forgotten reasons? And with

what half-remembered regrets?
Time was when spring's delirium fueled
the intensities of summer. Autumn

then added a melancholy strain as the
passion that once consumed the lovers now
consumed itself. And well before the first

snow fell, the lovers went their ways.
That's how the elders explained to us
the changing of the seasons.

Other stories taught us other lessons.
Odd how many of them followed the arc
of the seasons or a doomed affair.

It's as if our lives could still be measured
by the pastoral rhythms of seasonal change,
or the one that got away. It's an old song

with modern lyrics, noir lighting, rainy
nights watched through a steamy café window,
and the story that's about to unfold.

18.

A livelihood amounts to a slow death
when your passion and your labor are at odds.
When your daily bread is bitter, and

life has passed you by. Familiar stories
that bear repeating. Age diminishes
your usefulness to capital, and, they

would have you believe, to yourself. Yet,
they are happy who earn their living by doing
what they love. Hope for a better future

counters doubt that we'll live to see it.
Skeptics rattle every door with
a diligence born of cruel optimism.

Prepared for the worst, while hoping
for the best, albeit without expectations.
Given that life owes no one a living,

that would make us even. You might
well work your life away, but that's just
your day job. Your real work begins

when the tide returns and it's time
to fill in the blanks. Asked about sub-
sistence, the poet said, "No, thanks."

19.

His grief exceeded the very words for
which he had most use. Orphans, call them,
in light of their parentage, the dead

languages of gone worlds to which we
are indebted. Worlds in fragments
are romantically linked to the ruins

that recall for us a fictive Golden Age.
Not ours. Never ours. Always past.
Always elsewhere. The kind of place

we'll never be invited (and wouldn't be
at ease in if we were). The kind of place
where the right kinds of people say

the right kinds of things, *and* they look
good doing it. What's *not* a good look is
the wealth derived from genocide and

slavery. Wealth and privilege which only
exist at the expense of those who are far
from free. The caveat is, if the shoe fits.

Civility is strained by our discontents.
Consider those who are disenfranchised,
among whom none are counted as one.

20.

Regarding the deontological shuffle,
conscience bets on heads to win,
seeking to earn the remission of sins.

Where chasing dreams means fitting in,
assimilation is on the rise, and there
goes allegiance to your mother tongue.

Other people's rules, in other people's
words, replace the music in your ears.
Heads, and you know to trust your gut.

Tails, and you'll need some big magic
to liberate these songs. Art suffers
from commercial constraints. It's only

job is to pimp for consumption, to
include the caskets at Immanent Acres,
which will outlast fame's presumption.

Blind faith guided our very first steps.
Freedom was a ticket on the last bus out.
Confirmation bias was our bête noire.

Please leave the bottle and bring more
glasses. The band is coming back onstage
and the final set's about to begin.

21.

You're right to wonder where poems come from.
Outside a door marked "No Admittance,"
we could barely read when our quest began.

Given a back to every beyond, there's
an outside chance we'll live to tell of
our search for the source of our poems.

We looked where poetry seemed most likely.
Where words were our last best hope.
Where every time a caesura appeared,

they turned us back with a wave. And so it
went, each day the next. It was only in the
final draft the text ambushed the ending.

That must be when the editors panicked.
They found that by reordering the words
they made an ending they could live with.

Which has nothing to do with where
poems come from, nor does it even begin to
explain the workings of "other minds."

Those are topics for another day. Just as one
line leads to the next, we aim to follow
where language leads. Somebody say *Amen*.

22.

This is a poem about life among
the replicants, those you once knew as
friends and neighbors before they'd

been absorbed. Any path mapped out
by lovers will take the long way home.
It's as if you could live through your

own denouement. Such poems as these
are called *tombeaux*. Whose lines recall
your days among us and the work that

you left behind. When death is sudden,
there is no reprieve. Prolonged, and
it leaves too much time for reflection.

Jargon assigns a likely cause. Keywords
mandate the degree of difficulty. We
are just now seeing how aggressive it is.

The question isn't if, but when.
Left untreated, you'll remain intact,
but only for as long as you resist.

It's really all about staying on trend.
The Replicator will see to your end.
And you'll be the last of your line.

23.

Beyond the passages in this arcade
there lies the great unknown.
Sooner or later, we'll get there, but,

since the journey *is* the destination,
we're always already where we are.
Meanwhile, the replicants are busy

absorbing the locals (who have put up
scant resistance). Remarkably enough,
none decline or complain, largely

because they have since forgotten how.
In brief, replication selects for traits that
favor post-human efficiencies. Namely,

replicants who will meld with other
replicants and produce vast fortunes for
the Replicators. In other words,

humans did this to themselves. They
built the first replicants to break the
unions and thus increase their profits.

After much applause, the curtain fell.
The Dawn of the Replicants had opened
strong before an audience of replicants.

24.

As predicted, the sky fell. And decades
later, it's still falling, to which we have
grown accustomed. Multiple crises came

and stayed, never quite living up
to their billing, but never leaving, either.
Yet, for the brave, it did present

an unprecedented glimpse of what, if
anything, lay beyond our purview,
vast and verdant though it once was.

The old maps warn of monsters, which
were tropes for the unknown. And what
we don't know may indeed be harmful.

The obvious problem was how to
seek knowledge without collapsing
from the weight of our ignorance.

Which could be fatal, but some there
are who say you must die to be reborn.
That, of course, assumes you're game

for a lifetime of that much more of the
same. So you walk the Earth. And then
you don't. And in time, the sky changes.

25.

Some ironies arise in context.
Others are purely formal. Of all the
joints in Retroville, we ended

up at Kosmo's. Little more than a
hole in the wall, but it did have stars on
the ceiling and a well-oiled clientele.

We learned to fear what we read
in their faces, knowing we would
one day see it in ours. Whence,

our aversion to cheap booze, bright
lights, and mirrors. Decades after
our wastrel youth, we are reconciled

to the bad decisions that led us to
the flophouse of wisdom, right next
to death's front door. As you might

have expected, this has taken a toll. But
how tell the choosers from their choices?
Among today's more telling ironies are

the baskets beneath which we hide our
light. Not our decision, but we've been
assured that we have no place in the sun.

26.

Shadow words outline singularities.
Who looks for order within disorder
invokes big magic through repetition.

Inhale chaos. Exhale poetry. Tell us
only what you know to be true. Note
that the immaterial is tragic, more

than any human. When all they see
is what they know to look for, the life
of the mind is stifled. No blame, says

The Book of Changes. No blame at all,
says The-Way-That-Is-Not-One. Blame-
less, affirms the truth of inexistence.

To the living we pay homage to their
imperfections, the secret source of all
true beauty, as if we were made by hand.

Meanwhile, the search for order continues
amid the rubble of a ruined ethic,
overseen by the wraiths of childhood.

Order requires no regimentation.
That comes later with laws and statutes
and a longing for chaos and poetry.

27.

I've begun restoring the furniture music,
which has languished in the attic for decades.
My concerto for digital zither is complete.

Based on the game of musical chairs, when
a passage ends, the standing player leaves.
When the zither leaves, the concerto ends.

As encore, we offered silent variations on
a single minor chord. It was then that
the audience made for the street, eager to

recover its suspended disbelief and charging
the late-night air with menace as we headed
home from the gig. Albeit, with the barricades

in place, our block is unassailable. But no one
wants to live like this. It was different down
at the crossroads, the time we sold our souls.

Satan himself invented contract law.
Anyone who ever signed with him has
ended up in hell. Such is the price of

the ticket that will speed you on your way.
Remember to exercise all due caution when
you choose making poetry to fill your days.

28.

It's in the particulars. Storm clouds drift
over balding mountains, cold-filtered through
a gray-green motif. Where welcoming smiles

brought tears to our eyes, embraces that
had waited for decades followed. Exile
began with a youthful revolt. That's when

we first learned the taste of defeat.
Then, as we grew older and weak,
they deemed it safe to call us home.

Why bother? You might well wonder.
It's public relations, nothing more. The new
regime wants to show its compassion.

They say we're no longer a danger, even
to ourselves. Just a few old men
and the books they carried with them.

The old regime burned books for fun.
The new regime wants to read and learn
how we managed to survive in exile.

Admittedly, those were difficult years.
But now all we need are a jug and a loaf,
and we'll blueprint the *next* revolution.

29.

Decay is a dividend of cultural capital.
Ambient sounds impart mixed emotions.
Real time only counts birds in the hand.

I no longer know to whom I'm speaking.
A clear instance of actionable intel.
The rubric is, speak, so we can see you.

Inflated as a tyrant's dream, totality
has such a posthumous ring. Once more,
our assumptions have led us astray.

From the nanosphere to the multiverse,
we've gathered some big data. Now,
it's time to make those mathemes sing.

I must admit I can only recall past
moments of loss and humiliation, the sting
of betrayal and the lash of defeat.

Not what one hoped for, but so it went.
Albeit, there *have* been bright moments,
the dark times left their invisible scars.

These, the hallmarks of impossible poetry.
The herald of that which remains unsayable,
but aspires to be written one day.

30.

The poem's provenance was never in doubt.
Fragments stigmatized wayward sentences.
The thought police archived dissident verbs.

Right at the outset, vandals euphemized
what true believers call the sacred word.
It appears the vandals found a loophole

which permits tongues of fire to illumine
the text. Docile harmonies gave way
to dissonance. Tonality left the stage.

Discrepant lyrics provoked a riot.
Rotund demagogues frightened no one.
Well Met ghosted Hail and Farewell.

Bootleg identikits won best of show.
Traumatic memoirs, writ by gaslight,
scoffed at trinkets passing for art.

Now let's see some creative backlash.
To make art of pain is to say what you *know*
of your feelings, *not* what you feel.

It's a wicked adage, not a magic pill.
Poets write to think with their poems.
Their poems think what they will.

31.

Ghost tones yearn for object status.
Cold comfort seeks the warmth of suns.
Not for nothing means you're for sale.

Impediments call for work-arounds
where a brace of bots with artificial
brains are billed as coming attractions.

If the same lie is told a thousand times
is that one lie or a thousand? Does it
matter if you told a thousand people once

or a few friends over and over again
(and again, once more with feeling)?
When ghosts started leaving notes

in the lunchroom, they seemed to be
blurbs for a strange little book that
foretold the end of the world. And

which the poet, mentored by spirits,
had first foreseen as a child. Visions
he recorded in his youthful scrawl.

Memoirs are all the rage these days.
His details his youth fighting fascists,
The Armies of Armageddon.

32.

The poet was a poet before he was
a ghost. Before he was a poet, he was a
diffident child. This may account for

his saturnine views on the afterlife
and all its godly baggage. The smart
money bet on contingency and chance,

which guided his fingers on the keys.
His grail was to set the impossible poem
to no less impossible music. This

suggests he was bound to fail.
Although, à la Beckett, he would try
to "fail better." Simply stated,

we've seen what was possible. Note
Beckett's use of rubbish bins
to limn the ambit of his characters.

Imagine being trapped somewhere
with only your words for company and
your memories to ruin your sleep.

Then trade up to a single room and
you've captured the poet's modest life
from before he became a ghost.

33.

Keywords unleashed a storm of sources.
The thunder told us where we'd been, but
not where we were going. Our only choice

was to cleave to the coastline where
prehistory mocked the eternal present
and embraced the uncertain future.

Overtures presaged coming disasters.
Postapocalyptic nightmares were common.
A surfeit of hindrances defeated sleep.

One day, the storm will pass. We'll pick up
the pieces and solve the puzzle that brought
us to where the clocks have stopped and

the compass tilts in all directions except
the one that gets us home. Grave matters
need no translation. The life of the mind,

whatever else, is an epistemic adventure.
Picture a single room, barely furnished with
a bed, a table, a sink, and a chair.

In just such a room, his quest began.
After choosing dreams over waking
nightmares, the poet woke with a plan.

34.

Books belong in the public domain.
But only if the public will read them.
Though I don't really write for other

people, once I'm done, the books exist
for any willing reader. It's not unlike
learning a new language in order to speak

to the natives. "A new music is a new mind."
And if you're not looking for a change
of mind, you should probably book a cruise.

The natives of poetry are the words
of the poem. Attend them and what seems
like magic happens. Let it. And see

the world anew. But note, the natives
are indifferent to your needs. They bring
you news that has stayed news because

you've done nothing about it. The poem
can't offer food or shelter, peace or justice,
cash or a job. And asking that is folly.

In a confusion of categories – fire for ice –
the natives are restless and tired of
waiting for another throw of the dice.

35.

You bet the ranch and came up snake eyes.
The movie was better than your book.
Meanwhile, as seen from sea, the horizon

forms the gentlest arc, a matter of degrees.
Thus is it said, and wisely so, Nature is
always in good taste, even at its savage best.

The play, said the poet, begins with
the world, but it acquires a more personal
cast as its motley characters take

their turns – freelance graphemes
in search of a font. In the blue light
of a Paris evening, the patina

of beauty that comes with age
has endured much and learned little
from trafficking in appearances.

Back at the ranch, they sold your past
and left you no future to speak of.
Now you watch as the horizon recedes.

A widening gap that never closes.
Hence, your Sisyphean image of life
among the authors in eternity.

36.

Let's pretend it's *not* about the money.
That each of us has a clean, well-lighted place
where the air is fresh and the water pure,

the land fertile, and the food abundant.
Later, you can light out for parts unknown,
but for now be patient with your elders.

Hear them out when they tell their tales.
Pretend that their labors made a difference
and that they found another way forward

that *wasn't* about the money. Pretend
that we're not pretending, but are wanting
to change the world. Where to begin?

How best go about it? How can we
avoid making matters worse? It's true
that we'd rather avoid bloodshed,

but fascists *are* an ongoing blight
on the world, though they're not alone.
We have the numbers, if not the will,

to disarm nations, open borders,
feed the people, and transform
the economy – one pillar at a time.

37.

Now, as we near the end of the dance,
time resumes and soon overtakes
the years that led to this moment –

a duration we think of as timeless.
But *life* itself is just a matter of time. Says
the magus who first squared a circle.

Measure twice and cut once. It's the same
for a crib or a coffin. Or a single cord, cut by
Fate, for one who's left this mortal coil.

Most would agree. When it's time, it's time.
Few of us expect to get a second chance.
All we ever hoped for was one last dance.

Memorials are built upon one's net worth.
Me? I'll end in a pauper's grave, reserved
for intestate poets and sundry other knaves.

Where a bit of fame is worth a headstone,
a bit of gossip is worth another round.
More if the subject is still above ground.

At the wake, the mourners are lost in
thought, moved to reflect on their own
demise, at least till the booze runs out.

38.

There's not only no time *like* the present,
there's no time *but* the present to speak of.
When you conjure the past or envision

the future, is it not from the present
you inhabit? The present lasts almost
no time at all – a conundrum sustained

by sheer gumption (itself a source of
clean-burning energy, an affront to the
worship of the status quo, and a practice

measured in the hours spent huddled
with one line waiting for the next).
Of time, all we know are bits and pieces.

We know *kinds* of time, but not time as
such. Hence, as far as eternity is concerned,
the authors are right where they belong.

Of course, one hopes to join them one day,
but sheer gumption says there's work to be
done. And that will be done in the present

as you live it, or it won't be done at all.
There is, as Niedecker rightly observed,
"no lay off from this condensary."

39.

Striding smartly toward eternal silence,
willing to learn, but what? It's anyone's
guess, but for now it's yours alone.

When yesterday's odes arrive tomorrow,
who will recall their spectral glamor
or the steely emotions they inscribe?

And what are we to make of our new
reality? A gelid moon lights a minor
planet approaching its half-life and still

beautiful, even as human habitation
has exponentially despoiled the landscape,
fouled the air, polluted the water, and

warmed the planet by lethal degrees.
And still one seeks a place in that world,
a habitable place, if such exists, far from

the overplus that clogs the Earth and
continues to burgeon in real time.
Morning thunder gives voice to the heat.

But the rain (much needed) never arrives.
So the crops wilt, and the people starve,
and a white paper explicates everything.

40.

Walking with the dead in memory of
hours spent talking poetry along the
shore. How a raw east wind turned

the bay choppy, against the grain of the
outbound tide that would one day carry
him away. This, then, in memory of

old dreams, rich laughter, and decades
spent working in the dark. Even as he
dreamt of life after poetry, he chose to

stay the course. And it wasn't an easy
decision. Looking askance at schools and
trends, he welcomed his few, if querulous

friends to share the Spartan splendor of
his mind. Deaf to praise, he never learned
the truth. His work found readers that he

never knew. But what to make of that out-
bound tide? Every time it turns, its volume
increases. Where real losses cancel imaginary

gains, so, too, our losses, more each year,
until one day not a friend remains to share
some laughter and another round of beer.

41.

We ignored the early warning signs
until age came upon us. Now, after
learning to make accommodations,

we can manage the loss of a step.
Then, one day, it will be more than
a step. But why call dying "going

home" unless you were raised in
the suburbs? Imagine scouring your
second mind for a phrase to still

the restless dead. We'd miss the
grumblings we take for admonitions,
and we'd miss their unfiltered views

on life, albeit bittersweet. Given,
we'll join them soon enough, we're
already invisible to most observers.

Meanwhile, hustlers embrace their
acclaim, stoked by ersatz critics. Thus,
to secure a place in history for their

common sentiments, relatable syntax,
and all the little deprecations that reveal
their purblind sense of entitlement.

42.

We survived our cameos in their
death-driven dreams. Now, we
must look to dreams of our own,

albeit they are Postapocalyptic.
The end times didn't go well for us
till we mastered lucid dreaming.

We began to imagine a habitable
planet, with more on offer than
disposable diapers, microplastics,

and the indestructible cockroach.
Small wonder Einstein concluded
that imagination is more important

to human survival than knowledge.
Tell that to your sitting governments,
which, being of the political classes,

possess very little of either. Imagine
a compact between orbiting bodies,
the one you inhabit and the one you

created. In effect, a body of work.
Then, imagine that you're a free
agent in a world only you can see.

The Age of Reason

"To be or not to be. That's not really a question."
—Jean-Luc Godard

Based on newspaper and magazine articles
published between 1948 & 1955.

1.

Parker's Mood was rising up the charts. The sun was setting *a la cinco de la tarde*. Winter ushered in *The Birth of the Cool*. "It was a dark and stormy night."

—

Stalin persecuted "rootless cosmopolitans." Posters cautioned American citizens to "beware the enemy within." The Soviet Union's Berlin blockade was broken by an Allied airlift.

—

Newborns recognize their mothers' voices and coo to establish their own. They practice sitting, standing, and lying prone. Rocking in their cradles and learning how to roll.

—

Eliot won the Nobel Prize. Auden won the Pulitzer Prize. Publications included Pound's *Pisan Cantos;* Williams's *Paterson, Book II*, and Langston Hughes's *One-Way Ticket*.

—

Ajenian performed Cage's *Sonatas & Interludes*. Cowell's *Symphony No. 5* premiered, as did Bartok's *Viola Concerto*. Vinyl records went on sale, an acoustic revelation.

—

The Peekskill riots broke out. The Indo-Pakistan War ended in a stalemate and the division of Kashmir. Over 1,400 Black Americans were lynched between 1900 and 1950.

2.

Ghost writers haunted the airwaves. *The Third Man* won the Grand Prix at Cannes. The US Department of War was rebranded the Department of Defense.

—

The Soviets tested their first atomic bomb. The FBI named A-list celebrities as members of the Communist Party. A rhesus monkey named Al became the first primate in space.

—

Babies start babbling around six months. They are practicing the sounds of their mother tongue. They also practice laughing while they roll around on the floor.

—

Pound was awarded the Bollingen Prize. Neruda fled Chile through the Andes on horseback, with the manuscript of *Canto General* in his hand.

—

Birdland opened in New York City, the Lighthouse Café in Hermosa Beach, and the Black Hawk in San Francisco. Birdland was named for Charlie Parker, also known as Bird.

—

Soviet authorities deported more than 92,000 people from the Baltic states. South Africa banned mixed marriages. Cross-burnings proliferated throughout the American South.

3.

Kerouac coined the phrase "Beat Generation." Wile E. Coyote and the Roadrunner debuted in *Fast & Furry-ous*. Charge cards made their US debut, launching consumer debt.

—

The Suppression of Communism Act took effect in South Africa. Fuchs confessed he was a Soviet spy. Truman ordered development of the hydrogen bomb. The Korean War began.

—

After nine months of playing with sounds, babies put sounds together with rhythm and tone in ways that sound like normal speech. This is called the "jargon phase."

—

Publications included "Projective Verse" by Olson, *Auroras of Autumn* by Stevens, and *Collected Later Poems* by Williams. The Oppens went into exile.

—

The Cool School valued "clarity of expression; subtlety of meaning; emotion rather than emoting; progressive ambitions, and a tendency to experiment."

—

Apartheid began with the Group Areas Act. Separation of the races was modeled on American segregation. Two battalions of Viet Minh attacked a French base in French Indochina.

4.

Schuman proposed a pan-European union, a precursor to the EU. Congressional hearings on Organized Crime began. British spies Burgess and McLean defected to the USSR.

—

Forces from the Chinese Communist Party entered Beijing. The Stasi was created in East Germany. And the UN declared China an aggressor in the Korean War.

—

At twelve to eighteen months, babies begin speaking in one-word utterances (the holophrastic stage). The full range of vowels is produced well before that of consonants.

—

Corman founded *Origin*. Publications included *Paterson, Book IV* by Williams; *Montage of a Dream Deferred* by Hughes; *Collected Poems* by Moore, and *Cane* by Toomer.

—

Sonny joined Miles. The first US jazz festival took place. Alan Freed coined the phrase "rock and roll" to introduce R&B to a broader, predominately white audience.

—

Egypt demanded British troops leave the Suez Canal. China annexed Tibet. A petition describing genocide against African Americans was delivered to the United Nations.

5.

New film releases included *Superman and the Mole Men, Lost Continent, The Man from Planet X, The Day the Earth Stood Still, Thing from Another World,* and *When Worlds Collide.*

—

Einstein argued for the peaceful use of nuclear energy. The first thermonuclear device was tested. The Rosenbergs were sentenced to death.

—

At eighteen to twenty-four months, children speak in two-word phrases (the two-word stage). Clear syntactic and semantic relations begin to appear.

—

Lagerkvist won the Nobel Prize. Sandburg won the Pulitzer Prize. Stevens won the National Book Award. Ransom won the Bollingen Prize. Cummings won a Guggenheim.

—

Ives's *Symphony No. 2* premiered. Jukebox favorites included Parker's "Au Privave" and "Blues for Alice," Forrest's "Night Train," and Monk's "Straight, No Chaser."

—

The CPP won the national elections in the Gold Coast. The UN *Convention Relating to the Status of Refugees* was signed. The Nepalese revolution led to a democratic constitution.

6.

The Catcher in the Rye appeared. The active ingredients in the contraceptive pill were synthesized. Wildfires devastated the American West. Beckett published *Molloy*.

—

The Marshall Plan expired. It cost a few billion in today's dollars to rebuild Western Europe. Armistice negotiations began at Kaesong to end the Korean War.

—

At age two and a half, children progress to the "telegraphic stage" of speech. Utterances exhibit phrase structure and tend to follow the grammatical rules of the language.

—

O'Hara published *A City Winter*. Publication of "The Fight Against Formalism in Art and Literature, for a Progressive German Culture" outlined East Germany's cultural policy.

—

Thelonious Monk: Genius of Modern Music was the jazz Record of the Year. *The Rake's Progress* premiered in Venice. "Mona Lisa" won an Oscar for Best Song.

—

Libya gained its independence. In Sweden, an eighteen-year-old sailor was fined for "kissing in public." The Sri Lanka Freedom Party was formed.

7.

A *Streetcar Named Desire* opened in theaters. The first experimental nuclear power plant opened in Idaho. And the UN declared the first International Mother Language Day.

—

A coup restored Batista to power in Cuba. The US Army Special Forces were created. And East Germany announced formation of the National People's Army.

—

The post-telegraphic stage of speech begins around age three and continues into fully developed language skills, which children acquire around age six.

—

New World Writing first appeared. Publications included *Le Fou* by Creeley, *A Mask of Janus* by Merwin, *Collected Poems* by MacLeish, and *The Anathemata* by Jones.

—

The Modern Jazz Quartet was assembled. Les Paul introduced the solid-body electric guitar. Recent releases included *Bird and Diz* and *The Amazing Bud Powell*.

—

Nkrumah was elected Prime Minister of Gold Coast. Bolivia's National Revolution instituted universal suffrage, nationalized the mines, and enacted agrarian reform.

8.

The King is dead. Long live the Queen. The first successful sex reassignment surgery was performed. As was the first open-heart surgery. "Lawdy Miss Clawdy" climbed the charts.

—

The US tested the first hydrogen bomb. Adenaur survived an assassination attempt. The Soviet Union vetoed Japan's application for UN membership.

—

If we follow Vygotsky's theory, language and thought are intertwined. As a child's cognitive development continues to age twenty-five, so, too, does their linguistic capacity.

—

On the Night of the Murdered Poets, thirteen Soviet Jews, including several poets, were executed. Cummings was given a visiting professorship at Harvard.

—

Cage's composition *4'33"*, during which the performer does not play, premiered in Woodstock. Schaeffer published *In Search of Concrete Music*.

—

In Kenya, the Mau Mau Uprising put colonial powers on notice. Kenyatta was arrested for conspiring with the Mau Mau. Police in Bangladesh fired on marching students.

9.

Watson and Crick described the double-helix structure of DNA. Huxley experimented with mescaline. And the CIA approved LSD for use in illegal human experiments.

—

Stalin died. Khrushchev became General Secretary of the CPSU. The Asian Socialist Conference opened in Rangoon. The Korean War ended.

—

That humans have an innate capacity to learn language is now widely accepted. In question is whether there is a critical period within which to exercise that capacity.

—

Moore won the Pulitzer. Publications included the *Libretto for the Republic of Liberia* by Tolson; *six nonlectures* by Cummings; *In Cold Hell, In Thicket* and *Mayan Letters* by Olson.

—

The first International Summer School for New Music was held at Darmstadt. Elvis made his first records. *Jazz at Massey Hall* was released.

—

The Batepá massacre saw hundreds of native Creoles, known as *forros*, massacred in São Tomé by the colonial administration and Portuguese landowners.

10.

Transsexual Christine Jorgensen returned to New York and became a nightclub performer. Mary Martin was *Peter Pan.* And Gary Cooper spoke sparingly as high noon approached.

—

The CIA helped overthrow Mosaddegh in Iran. The Soviet Union tested a thermonuclear device. The UN rejected the People's Republic of China's petition for membership.

—

And *feral* children? Is their language ability lost because the critical period is passed? Have their brains developed differently so that thought and language are forever separated?

—

Churchill won the Nobel for Literature. Publications included Stein's *Bee Vine Time and Other Pieces* and Baldwin's *Go Tell It on the Mountain.* *Waiting for Godot* premiered.

—

Sinatra began recording at Capitol Records. Hank Williams recorded "Your Cheatin' Heart." A pioneering electronic music studio opened in Cologne at station NWDR.

—

Kenyatta was sentenced to seven years in prison. France agreed to the provisional independence of Cambodia – and ousted King Mohammed V of Morocco.

11.

Lord of the Flies was published in London. The words "under God" were added to the Pledge of Allegiance. Eisenhower warned against intervention in Vietnam.

—

Einstein warned that nuclear war could lead to mutual annihilation. The US tested a hydrogen bomb and launched the first nuclear-powered submarine.

—

Can we have language without thought attached? Can we have thought without language? Or does the lack of development in either one prevent development in the other?

—

Creeley founded *The Black Mountain Review*. Publications included *The Desert Music* by Williams, *The Fables of La Fontaine* by Moore, and *Collected Poems* by Stevens.

—

Moses und Aron premiered in Hamburg. The Newport Jazz Festival was founded. The first Fender Stratocaster was produced in Southern California.

—

The First Indochina War ended with North Vietnam, South Vietnam, Cambodia, and Laos emerging victorious against the French Army. War in Algeria was ramping up.

12.

Eisenhower delivered his "domino theory" speech. The Viet Minh were reorganized as Viet Cong. Dulles said Indochina was not essential to the security of Southeast Asia.

—

The Soviet Union recognized the sovereignty of East Germany. Dulles accused Communist China of sending combat troops to Indochina to train Viet Cong guerrillas.

—

A language requires a semantic dimension. And meaning is its Grail. A poem is a structure of cause and consequence. What goes unspoken goes unheard.

—

Roethke won the Pulitzer. Aiken the National Book Award. Auden the Bollingen Prize. Publications included *Poems 1923–1954* by Cummings and *Poems 1947–1954* by Kees.

—

Miles released *Blue Haze*. Blakey released *A Night at Birdland*. Monk recorded *Blue Monk*. Sonny recorded "Airegin." And the Brubeck quartet went to college.

—

The Mau Mau leader Itote was captured. The US Supreme Court in *Brown v. Board* ruled against racial segregation in public schools. The Algerian War of Independence began.

13.

Blackboard Jungle premiered. Its soundtrack unleashed the rock-and-roll era. Teens constituted a vast new market. In-N-Out Burger opened the first drive-through restaurant.

—

The Warsaw Pact was signed. Free movement between North and South Vietnam ended. The US began developing intercontinental ballistic missiles armed with nuclear warheads.

—

The five stages of literacy development include emergent literacy, alphabetic fluency, words and patterns, intermediate reading, and advanced reading.

—

Johnson published *The Poems of Emily Dickinson* in three volumes. The Six Gallery Reading, where Ginsberg first read "Howl," spotlighted the Beats and the San Francisco scene.

—

The Prophetic Herbie Nichols debuted. Monk released *Thelonious Monk Plays Duke Ellington*. Miles formed his First Great Quintet. Charlie Parker died.

—

The Montgomery Bus Boycott began. The Freedom Charter of the anti-apartheid South African Congress Alliance was adopted. Emmet Till was lynched in Money, Mississippi.

14.

Catholicism held that at seven a child had reached the age of reason and was morally accountable for their thoughts, words, and deeds. *Rebel Without a Cause* was a box-office hit.

—

War began between North and South Vietnam. The U-2 spy plane made its first flight. In case of nuclear attack, children were taught to assume the blast position beneath their desks.

—

Jakobson said the poetic function forces readers to focus on the signifiers in linguistic signs, away from the signifieds. This it does by superimposing similarity on contiguity.

—

Publications included *Journey to Love* by Williams, *All That is Lovely in Men* by Creeley, *Pictures of the Gone World* by Ferlinghetti, and *The Dissolving Fabric* by Blackburn.

—

Boulez premiered *Le Marteau sans maître*. The International Society for Contemporary Music Festival took place in Baden-Baden. Johnny Cash released *Folsom Prison Blues*.

—

Rosa Parks energized the Civil Rights Movement. Hundreds were killed in anti-French rioting in Morocco and Algeria. Global empires trembled. There was freedom in the air.

Endgame

"In the landscape of extinction,
precision is next to godliness."
—Samuel Beckett

1.

"What to do? And what to do *next*?" I raise these questions as evidence
that doing isn't done. Though I hesitate to put forward answers – and
have yet to speak of my intentions. No one *means* to circulate their
blood. But say I wanted to write a poem. Poetry is more than wanting to.
As desire rises from the ashes of defeat, it infiltrates our dreams. Hence,
we are fated to search for meaning (as if *to do* were *to mean*).

2.

Meaning is as meaning does. And what it does is inscribe itself in the
annals of transient thought. "He wants to say his life is real. No one
can say why." It's been years since he first heard that life is a search
for meaning. Real poems include real lemons, hanging from real trees.
But they can't include the accursed poet, whose practice follows where
language leads in the process of making his desire legible.

3.

Desire is mute in the face of disaster. The exile accepts his lot with
grace. His fate is to vanish without a trace. He enjoys sovereignty over
the badlands where he is expected to live out his days. Due east lies a
real desert. To the west lies the Desert of the Real. The former, a xeric
landscape; the latter noted for its toxic appeal. In the book of life, beset
by age, the exile is ready to turn the page.

4.

The magus offered sage advice. Peace, if it comes, will exact a price. From the earliest stirrings of your latent desire to the last words inscribed on the flag of your becoming, the Void awaits your return. If you can grasp how it is (*comment c'est?*), then you can grasp (*eo ipso*) why it matters. As well, there's the weight of the past you never wanted, the life you never had, and the expectations (there are always expectations) that await the coming of peace.

5.

The page is gravid with possibility, only to be humbled by the actual weight of words, seeming to arrive from out of nowhere. Tourists wonder at the poem's meaning. They assume it's theirs for the taking. An extended trope touts parts as wholes. Analysts rate these as high-value targets. The poem begins and ends with the world, wherever the flag of pain's unfurled. Making things plain to the poet's brain so that he's able to write once again.

6.

Form keeps pace where meaning falters. Memory retains far more than it admits. The image *du jour* seeks shade amid the ruins. Even now, there are far more treasures than days remaining to enjoy them. The poet searches the meanwhile for signs of the poem at the end of time. There is no infinity of blue to ponder. No all-seeing eye to appease. There *are* no other words but these.

7.

The annals of garden lore reveal that the serpent's wiles prevailed. And talk of obedience distracts from the pursuit of knowledge and the first assertion of free will, replete with consequences. Under the aegis of an angry god, the patriarchy flourished. But what of the serpent, the first of his kind? Was he not a teacher (this Mephitic creature)? He introduced Eve to the life of the mind. She found the core bitter, much like the rind.

8.

The black flag of rebellion was shredded, but still remained aloft. The bell tower tolled the final hour. It was time for the people to reclaim their power. Endless conflict was not a metaphor. Generations rose and fell. Thus did the One begin its struggle to make lasting peace with the Many it comprises, each singular, each transient, each presently absorbed in the news. "And the news is war as always."

9.

After weekend drives in the countryside to watch the seasons passing – and moonlit nights on the front-porch swing in the velvet dark of summer – we took to the rhythms of rural life, far removed from the endless hustle and buzz of the sleepless city. Some few dwell in eternal spring, while others inhabit our minds. There, amid the scent of impossible bouquets is the hell that shelters our losses. For us, the past is a walk in the graveyard. The present, at best, a passing fancy. And the future but a rumor on the wind.

10.

Where ageless verses set the scene, we bow to our antecedents. Belated, but emboldened by the words we're given, we seek the poem at the end of time. Lost souls gather in the Forest of Forgetting. Dead souls sing of the world they've forsaken. Whose former lives were spent on the run, as if to escape from life's zero sum. But what would any among them give for one more day in the sun?

11.

To war with yourself is to tilt at mirrors. Successive selves are all you've got, randomized shards of shed identities, back from hell for a curtain call and a spray of long-dead roses. While each of the many clings to the myth of a stable, eternal self. As if they could put death back on the shelf. What we know of dying we have learned from the dead. About whom my elderly uncle said, "At least they ain't gettin' any older."

12.

The grand jury voted the spirit of the law, more than its application. Theirs was an homage to karmic justice more than a verdict for stealing time. The accused was alleged to have added years to the lives of advocates for peace – years that he allegedly stole away from the violent in our midst. While legal experts brandished their theories, the jurors declined to indict. As the foreperson said in her churchical way: "It's not for us to know the hour or the day."

13.

Multiple sources say the test results correlate with predictions of confirmation bias. Once the cow jumped over the moon, the poet got some sleep. Then he woke to roll the stone for which no app exists. Whose previous job was counting stars by daylight. That was yet another dead-end gig. But proof that when his name's on the line, he'll show up ready to roll the dice and take what comes as a sign.

14.

Where "indefiniteness is an element in the true music," particulars are subject to loss of context. Strict definitions are off the table. And constant change is all we know. Where last chances languish in period chairs, a gaggle of poets lingers there, waiting for their luck to change. The desire for selfhood is a sign of lack. "The self is no mystery." It's a cul-de-sac. One with no exit but the one you took in search of the true music.

15.

Exit music is premature. You're still quite far from home. Footprints follow you wherever you go. Dead-ends tell you what you need to know. The person you are is the only impediment to the person you would become. So you seek the truth by looking askance. Without it, you're condemned to roam. And when you dream, you'll dream alone. You turned to art for clarity, but words can be so cruel. Then you wake to another day – a day in the life of a fool.

16.

Words without context are homeless warriors. Given: Earth is sorely wounded. Given: It will recover without us. Given: In the future, wars will be fought over arable land and fresh water. Given: Our history was written in blood. Our love of words will not suffice in the face of cataclysm. What's the point of preaching to the choir? When was the last time you had someone's back? Ran toward danger without thought for yourself? And spoke on behalf of the freedoms we lack? Honor who choose their words with care and send them against the dissembling air.

17.

I have dreamt the names of the disappeared, whom death has taken beneath its wing. And even as their numbers mount, their memory peoples my sleep. Free-floating letters, like tongues of flame, coalesce into arcane embers, seeking translation into poetry. Hence, these memos from the dead to the dying, whom they consider friends. We think we know them because we knew them. But, that is only as they were and will never be again.

18.

From revelation to centrifugal thought, a through line points the way. The *prima materia* is with us still. We drink ancient rainwater, bask in sunlight, and sleep under long-dead stars. Such are our links to the first of our kind – whose very bones have been enshrined. Perhaps our eventual extinction might be seen as a form of suicide. But remember, we're made of stardust, and there are solar winds to ride.

19.

After the sun's beneficence, nightfall brings a toxic mix of bad memories and worse dreams. White nights find him writhing in the sheets, only to rise, weary and worn, to begin another day. The poet's first client wants amatory verses with which to woo a woman called Edna (from the Hebrew word for *pleasure*). And the next client wants a crown of sonnets to celebrate a life of wedded bliss. He said the secret to a happy marriage is to end each day with a passionate kiss.

20.

Broken connections have real world impact. The gist of his memoirs prompted some strife. In light of which, it's clear the siesta is the sine qua non of civilized life. Where footnotes glossed the shards of his youth, appendices sullied his rep. Early reviews were contentious. His critics queried his every step. Bad blood led to words of rue. Passionately rendered, albeit rarely true.

21.

Their legacy of privilege is under review, but remains no less toxic for that. Where ideology is preferred to competence (thus to excuse their indolence), there's scant regard for the public good. Perpetual crisis is their only season. They balk in debate at the use of reason. Which leaves it to us to reverse the curse. Those best placed to improve the world have only made it worse.

22.

Imagine yourself in a world of words, and assume there's no way out. Assume that your future, once in doubt, was always already at hand. Assume your words will mean what they say and that you will be as you are. Note that the endgame starts right here. Where unbidden memories bear your losses, you come to accept your fate. We sought and found your fulgent word in the Forest of Regrets, a vast reserve where all your works lay on the shelves in state.

23.

She said, "I'm a writer, not a poet. I don't want all those words in my head." In this distinction, worthy of note, lies a motive we understand. An exorcism with precedent. And a legacy held on remand. Thus, these verses in defense of a poem that won't explain itself. Even as it stands at the ready, unopened on your shelf. We've dodged the flotsam of interpretation and the shoals of paraphrase. But of what use will our words be when we reach the end of our days?

24.

Tropism powered the turn to language. The image repertoire was past its prime. And the flag of necessity had been remade as a banner of pure possibility, under whose aegis we abjure politicians and all their puppeteers. After analysis parses our options, the answer lies in the act. Failure being endemic to poetry, we seek to fail better. Hence, the poet, a perpetual beginner, proceeds *as if* his work has just begun.

25.

Why think to begin again, unless in wonder to approach a frame within which words appear? Nothing he hasn't seen before, but still, it seems miraculous. Writing is more than a passion with him and death the only cure. Time passed without thought of dying. Immortal youth his only shield against every mortal threat. Then, one day, he fell in love. Life became precious. His lover, dear. And death became his greatest fear.

26.

As time's passage measures space, margins frame a virtual page, based on the Golden Section. It is in that light that words appear to render the text in situ – a singular pattern, which we call poetry, even though it *looks like* poetry. But this is not charades. When poems emerge from between covers, the message at last breaks free. But it's only for those with eyes to hear and ears to parse these songs of degrees.

27.

The form book on poetry gives long odds, regardless of your intentions. What to do is one question. Why you do it is another. And the latter amounts to failing better, the only constant in your writing life. That's when words must assert themselves, seeking to become articulate. Withal they disdain what *you* think to say. It's likely they find it absurd. Hence, you have to come to grips with "the heartlessness of words."

28.

It wasn't silence that greeted the poem, but the vacuum left in its wake.
The next day only brought more explanations. There can be no sound
without an atmosphere. Hence, there is no music of the spheres. No
voice from the heavens. No choir of angels. At the moment, there are
only the fading lines of the poem you thought you'd never forget. When
thought bubbles burst, they send forth blossoms, whose beauty leaves
you in their debt.

29.

How much credence shall we give to these relics of a snow-blind decade?
The past was rife with bad juju. Truth itself was an early victim in a
deadly war of attrition. At the end of your days, your truth dies with you.
Your memory will fade from the minds of friends. But, for now, you're
the steward of your words and the poems that bear them into the world
– after decades of good faith, sitting with them in the dark.

30.

A year of miracles stretched to include a bounty of well-tuned crystals.
A nailhead glinted on the workshop wall in a splash of morning light.
Thus, to excavate being is to expose its material base. Trust no claims
for any beyond that doesn't end with inexistence. From radio silence
to musical highs, we once tuned into Dolphy in Denmark, running the
changes on "Angel Eyes."

31.

Dusk settles on the bitter city. Long shadows mask the filth. The locals have no use for ornament. The old men wear old hats. The old women chat and plump their breasts, an old-world custom that charmingly persists. As historic buildings yield to the new, a forest of glass and steel towers plunges the streets into deepest shade. The result is a maelstrom of wind and detritus, through which embittered crowds must pass.

32.

Portraits like this are easy to come by. The hapless subject occupies the foreground, backgrounded by the city at night, replete with its signature skyline. He'd be more comfortable in his cubicle at work, if not the bar where he drinks his lunch. Instead, he's on a plein-air set, trying to look like he belongs and doing his neighbor, the painter, a solid. The painter assures him he looks like a native, grimly defiant in defeat.

33.

Not to disparage city life, whose denizens crowd the diner at dawn. But a sufficiency of microaggressions serves to establish the tenor of the day. Against which acts of human kindness are buffers that make life possible. The poet despairs of gentrification. Neighborhoods lost to urban pioneers. Orishas replaced with Michelin stars. And tenements ginned up as luxury condos, whose former tenants sleep on the street.

34.

They wanted you to taste of the world, but forgot to let you breathe. Tainted love impaired your song and never gave you time to grieve. When, at last, the future arrived, its annals were full of gaps. And that's why the text could only marvel at all the time elapsed. In the analogy, Earth is the text whose borders we failed to defend. We, who have failed in our duty of care to prevent our premature end.

35.

The lunar cycle is known by its phases. The poet is no less deliberate. His own phases range from rage to resignation. The one, inarticulate. The other, silent as the grave. While he drinks his coffee, he reads the news. "And the news is war as always." The last hard frost says change is coming. Winter passes like a world-weary ghost. Only to recall a favorite verse: "spring can really hang you up the most."

36.

High on a scaffold of pure conjecture, we apply fresh paint to an old conundrum – "Where do you get your language?" Restive thought knows many ways to circumvent its solution. Note that our practice is indivisible from the forms our poems assume. Not as vessels waiting to be filled, but as finite limits where phrases translate into vectors of thought, emblems of desire, lines of song and pure rhythmicity, one word at a time.

37.

Giant steps, by slow degrees, led us straight to the Court of Inquest, where death by misadventure was the verdict du jour. Otherwise known for their ingenuity, human error is their defining trait. It's the source of all beauty and most hard truths. For one thing, "No one listens to poetry." For another, this is edge-work. No net, no ball, no racquet. "Much wrong. A little rightness." Tasked with seeking the discrepant word, the poet will not be deterred.

38.

Blues people speak of trouble in mind. Who sang of the need for public justice. Marched to bring forth public justice. Suffered for want of public justice. And died at the hands of a grave injustice, a bitter irony indeed. Thus, do demagogues continue to thrive and spew their famous bootstrap jive. From each purveyor of goods or services to each according to their ability to pay. Thus does injustice dictate the terms by which every demon has its day.

39.

The root chord is chimerical. You can't go home again. The first inversion is empirical. A matter of using your senses. The second inversion is geodesic, subject to triangulation. The third inversion lands on a flatted fifth, which is called the devil in the music. When resolution faced dissolution, tonality sought to reclaim its throne. Once installed, it kept the peace by throwing the vanguard scraps and bones.

40.

Between the many and the one, who will not repeat their opinions for the inexistent pleasure of their company, there is no city distinct from its languages. Not least, the language of wizards – masters at marketing soul to the soulless and ephemera to those with imaginary deficits. Poets have no truck with wizards who prey on folks sans pity. *Bitter* is the word most often used to describe the roots of the city.

41.

Party politics is empty promises mired in partisan preferment. Some people seek proximity to power; some its acquisition. The former model the banality of evil. The latter a lack of moral imagination. Whenever they invoke the public good, their syntax, replete with platitudes, lies. And the dumber they get, the more they reflect the State they have crafted in their image.

42.

Poetry is not a form of madness. Nor are "things" what they're said to be. Visible light proves next to nothing as we map the city of dreams. Sleep, when it's not a torment, is a pleasure, much like love itself. In whose light, I'm nothing more than my other sees and says. False propositions seek to patch the crumbling arcades of our discontent, which, as friends are quick to assure us, only exists in our minds.

43.

And so it is as the old sage says, you can't drown twice in the same river. Inspired, no doubt, by "the more severe Muses," it's enough to recall the improbable setting of the very first poem he wrote. Alone at his desk, he recalls the paper on which unbidden words appeared *as if* he himself had typed them, straight from his brain to the page. Even then, the boy knew better. And even now, a lifetime later, he still hasn't changed his mind.

44.

Bare interior. Gray light. The journey is almost over. A procession of ghosts drifts past the window. A dumbshow of names and once familiar faces, all but lost to memory. Their banner reads, "All things are derived from their Genius." For what is thought without an object? The ghosts say words are the currency of fools, even as the poem says otherwise. Bare interior. Gray light. The journey is almost over.

46.

Our mounting losses diminish our gains. The passing of friends and comrades continues, as do these orphaned poems. This is no ode to immortality. No flag of truce to the culture industry. Instead, it's the torch we carry for our fate, even as the endgame approaches. The old poet pushed through his dementia and whispered: "*Work*. Do your work. You have to outlive the bastards."

TED PEARSON was born and raised on the San Francisco peninsula, a seventh-generation Californian. After early musical training, he began writing poetry in 1964, and subsequently attended Vandercook College of Music, Foothill College, and San Francisco State University. In 1976, he published his first book, *The Grit* and began his long association with the San Francisco Language Poets. He has since published over thirty books of poetry. He co-authored *The Grand Piano*, a ten-volume experiment in collective autobiography. He edited a posthumous edition of Craig Watson's last poems, *Epilogue*. And he co-edited *Bobweaving Detroit: The Selected Poems of Murray Jackson*. His essays have appeared at intervals since 1975. He lives in Northampton, Massachusetts.

www.ingramcontent.com/pod-product-compliance
Lightning Source LLC
Chambersburg PA
CBHW011145070726
47591CB00016B/2394